THE ONE AND ONLY COMMON SENSE SERIES

S0-FQX-722

From Beads to Bank Notes
The Story of Money

by Neale S. Godfrey

Illustrated by Randy Verougstraete

Modern Curriculum Press
Parsippany, New Jersey

To my children, Kyle and Rhett:

I listen to you. I learn from you. I trust you. I admire you.

But most of all I love you.

Mom

Editorial assistance provided by Pubworks, Inc.

Design: Rosanne Guararra

All photographs by Silver Burdett Ginn (SBG) unless otherwise noted.

3: *bkgd.* Texas A&M Early Childhood Development Center. 4: Erich Lessing/Art Resource, NY. 9: Amos Nachoum/Corbis Corporation. 10: *bkgd.* Superstock; *l.* E.R. Degginger/Color-Pic, Inc.; *r.* Phil Degginger/Color-Pic, Inc. 11: *clockwise from t.l.* American Numismatic Association/Tom Stack & Associates; Laurie Platt Winfrey, Inc.; The Granger Collection, New York; The Granger Collection, New York; The Granger Collection, New York; Lee Boltin/Boltin Picture Library; Laurie Platt Winfrey, Inc. 14: *l.* American Numismatic Association/Tom Stack & Associates; *r.* Giraudon/Art Resource, NY. 17: Laurie Platt Winfrey, Inc. 18: *t.* Matt Bradley/Tom Stack & Associates; *b.l.* Lee Boltin/Boltin Picture Library; *b.r.* American Numismatic Association/Tom Stack & Associates. 19: *l.,r.* American Numismatic Association/Tom Stack & Associates. 20: American Numismatic Association/Tom Stack & Associates. 21: *t.,b.* American Numismatic Association/Tom Stack & Associates.

Modern Curriculum Press
An Imprint of Pearson Learning
299 Jefferson Road
Parsippany, NJ 07054

ISBN 0-7652-1765-1

6 7 8 9 10 CA 06 05 04 03 02 01 00

What *is* money anyway? Sure, you use it all the time. But do you really know what it is? And for that matter, where it comes from? And how long it has been around? What did people do before there was money? We see and use money so often that we don't even think about it. But every once in a while it's a good idea to stop and wonder, "What *is* the real story behind money?"

Welcome to *From Beads to Bank Notes: The Story of Money*. This book will help you discover the answers to these questions and many others. But *From Beads to Bank Notes: The Story of Money* is more than just a history book. It will also teach you about how we make money and spend money. And, most of all, it will teach you the importance of saving and budgeting your own money.

Saving, spending, sharing, and planning for the future are important skills that you will need as you grow older. Money itself is neither good nor bad. It is what is done with money that counts. *From Beads to Bank Notes: The Story of Money* will help you discover how much fun understanding money can be.

Neale S. Godfrey

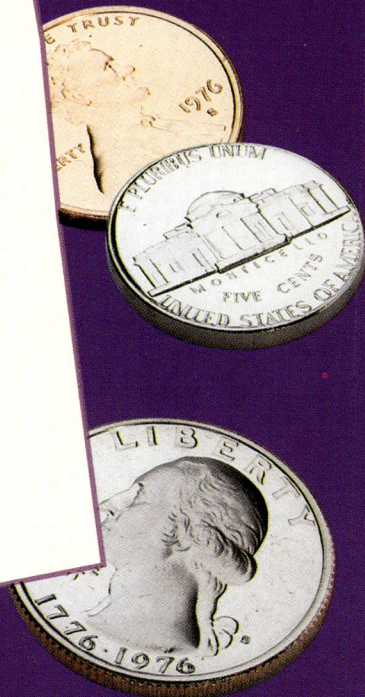

Contents

Chapter 3 It's Your Money! 29

Chapter 1

Money
Who Needs It?

We all do! **Why?**
It's part of our everyday **life**.
How did it all **start?**

Set your clock back 10,000 years. You're living in the days of the earliest people. You live in a cave or a shelter you built by yourself or with the help of your family. You eat whatever you are able to catch or find. You wear clothing made from animal skins. You have simple needs. You don't need much to survive. You certainly don't need money. After all, where would you spend it? There are no stores!

When did money come into the picture? Who invented it—and why? While we're on the subject, what is money, anyway?

You'll find the answers to these and many other questions in the pages that follow.

1

Introducing

Money
It's a Necessity

Can you imagine life without **money**? How would you pay for food, clothing, and shelter? Could you go to the movies? Could you buy a CD? Without money, you probably wouldn't survive very well!

Money isn't everything. A lot of great things are free. You don't need money to see a full moon or a colorful sunrise. You don't need money to have friends. You don't even need money to have fun! But in today's world, you need enough money to get by, to satisfy some of your needs.

You need money to buy **goods**, such as food and clothing. You need money to pay for a place to live or to travel on a bus or a train. You need money to pay for **services** provided by doctors and dentists.

Think about it. You need money for just about everything.

A Penny for Your Thoughts
Is money always valuable? Suppose you were on a desert island. What good would a suitcase of money be? What would you rather have instead?

Word Bank

money *anything a group of people accept in exchange for goods and services*

goods *real items, such as cars, wristwatches, and clothing*

services *work that is done for other people*

2

. . . Money!

Everybody Pitches In

It takes more than an allowance and your family's money to buy all the goods and services you need to survive. Your town or city also spends money for your benefit. It pays for things, such as playgrounds and police protection. Even the government spends money on you by paying for things such as teachers, schools, and highways.

Where does the money for all this come from? These goods and services are paid for with taxes—money collected from people and businesses. No single person pays for such things alone. What other things are paid for by money collected by your town, city, or state?

Have you heard some of these names that people have given money?

bread, bucks, greenbacks, sawbucks, lucre, cash, ace, deuce, boodle, spondulicks, simoleons, shekels, mazuma, vishneggles, the ready, rhino, palm oil, long green, dinero, jack, cabbage, scratch, dough, lolly, oof, gelt, chips, beans, bits, berries, spot, bob, quid, yard, skins, lettuce

3

What a Deal!

It's a Long Story

What happened? How did we go from not having money to needing money for almost *everything*? One thing is for sure. It didn't happen overnight.

Thousands of years ago, people lived where they could find food. Groups of people often moved from place to place, looking for food. They would sometimes follow large herds of animals. Usually groups could not stay in one place too long, because the food supply would run out.

A Matter of Fact

The word *money* comes from the Latin word *moneta*, which was the name of the place in ancient Rome where money was first made and stored.

Cave painting of people on the move

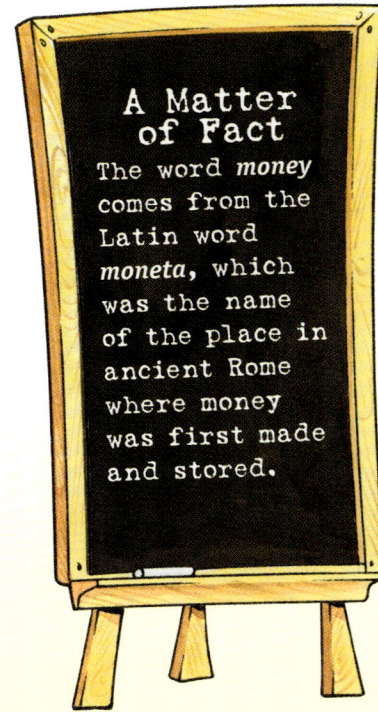

Hello There, Stranger!

Though people moved around a lot, they still didn't see or know much about the world. They probably had no idea what was going on across the sea or beyond the next big mountain. There were no books, no newspapers, and no TVs. Imagine living then!

Sometimes, one group of people would meet another group and see new things—new things they wanted. Remember a time you saw something new you wanted? Groups might trade with one another. One group might trade animal skins for fish that the other group had just caught. This sort of trade made it easier for both groups to get what they needed or wanted.

4

Settling Down

Moving from place to place can be very difficult, especially when you have to move everything you own, including your home. Some people decided to stay in one place. They had to find new ways to get food. They started farming. They learned how to grow plants for food and raise farm animals. Now people could stay in one place and have all the food they needed!

Soon, individual farms grew into small towns, and small towns grew into larger ones. In these large towns, not everyone needed to help grow the food. There was more time to spend on other things. So people developed other skills or crafts. Along with farmers, there were now carpenters and blacksmiths, weavers and potters, bakers and butchers. What other types of skills do you think might have been needed?

A Penny for Your Thoughts

Suppose one day a month was a "no money" day. If you had to barter for everything you'd need on that day, what goods or services would you trade? What makes a fair trade?

Word Bank

barter *trading goods or services with someone for different goods or services, without using money*

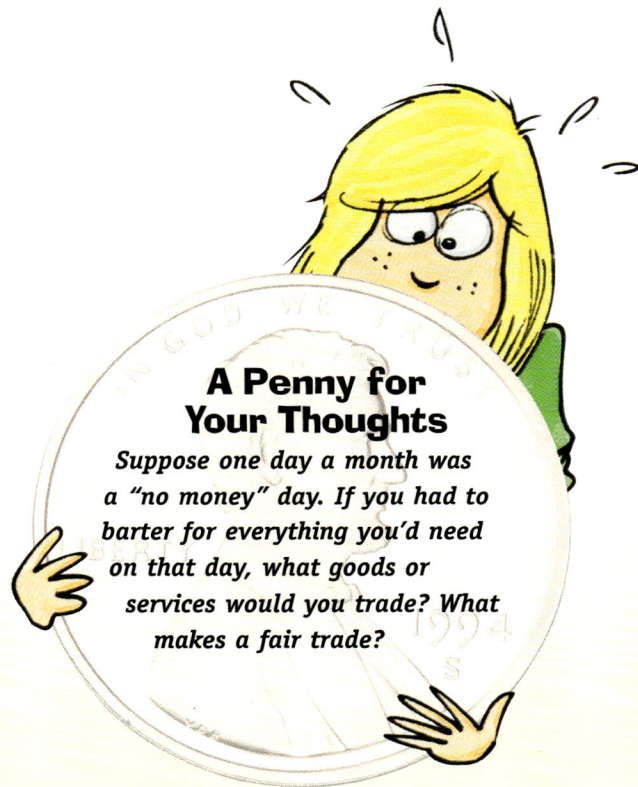

To Market, to Market

Farmers and craftspeople couldn't use everything they made or grew so they began to trade goods. A loaf of bread might be traded for some cloth. Pottery could be traded for grain. A carpenter might repair a wagon in exchange for some tools. This kind of trading is called **bartering**. People traded things they had for things they wanted or needed.

But still, no money was involved. Money—the coins and bills we use to pay for goods and services—had not yet been invented!

Let's Go Swapping

Through bartering, people were able to get many things they needed and wanted. Merchants would sometimes travel to faraway places and bring back things made or grown in these places. People would then trade their local items for goods brought from far away. People, tribes, even different countries bartered with one another.

It's Still Going On

In some countries, people still barter instead of using money. Some countries even barter with each other. For example, countries that grow wheat can barter with countries that produce sugar. Kids barter all the time. Exchanging baseball cards, stickers, or snacks—it's all bartering.

Let's Make a Deal

Bartering was easy as long as there were only a few things to barter. People agreed on what could be traded for what. But when there were hundreds of items to swap, it got very complicated. If someone wanted a tent but only had three camels, he'd have to find someone who was willing to exchange a tent for three camels. Sometimes, people traded for something they didn't want in the hope they could later trade it for something they *did* want.

A Fair Trade?

Sometimes, people didn't agree on what things were worth. For example, how many monkeys should one barter for a canoe? How many coconuts? Which was worth more—monkeys or coconuts? What if the person with the canoe had other ideas? Plus, people had to carry around everything they wanted to barter with—and that got very difficult. Bartering got so complicated that people looked for an easier way to trade.

A Penny for Your Thoughts

In colonial times, people sometimes wanted to come to America but didn't have enough money for the boat fare. They would offer to work for seven years for anyone who would pay their way across the ocean. These workers were called indentured servants. Do you think they got a fair deal?

A Matter of Fact

Sometimes parents who wanted their daughter to marry a certain man would offer the man their daughter plus valuable goods, such as land or a cow. Sometimes it worked the other way around. A man had to give the woman's parents something valuable in order to be allowed to marry her. This still happens in some countries today.

In the Beginning . . .

It's About Value

Bartering became difficult because it was not easy figuring out and agreeing on the **value** of things. You can tell the value, or worth, of something by knowing what people are willing to give you in exchange for it. If someone were to give you two apples for one orange, the value of an orange would be equal to two apples. When people bartered, they needed to agree on the value of their possessions. Otherwise, they could not agree on a trade!

It's Common Cents

Instead of bartering or trading with each other, people sometimes used a medium of exchange. The **medium of exchange** was used as a common measure of value. For instance, if shells are the agreed-upon medium of exchange, the value of everything is measured in shells. Everything is paid for in shells. A hat may cost five shells, a pair of shoes may cost fifteen shells, and a coat may cost fifty shells. Whatever is bought is paid for in shells. With an agreed upon medium of exchange, buying and selling is a lot easier. Why do you think this is true?

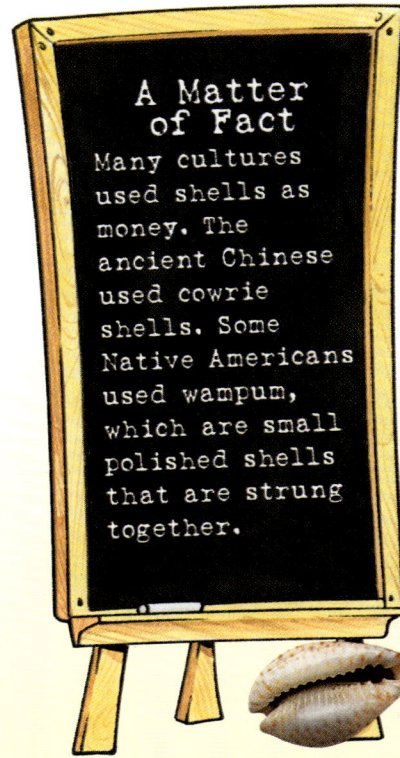

A Matter of Fact

Many cultures used shells as money. The ancient Chinese used cowrie shells. Some Native Americans used wampum, which are small polished shells that are strung together.

cowrie shells

How do people decide how valuable something is?

It depends. If you were thirsty, the value of something to drink would increase.

Word Bank

value the worth of something as measured in goods, services, or a medium of exchange

medium of exchange anything that a group of people agree has a certain worth

8

Money, Money Everywhere

Different people around the world used different things for money. In many parts of the world, salt was used as a medium of exchange. Salt was valuable because it was needed to preserve and flavor food. It was also valuable because it was hard to find. Other items that have been used for money around the world include tea leaves, shells, feathers, barley, seeds, camels, dried fish, elephant tail bristles, and even dead rats! Just about anything you can think of has probably been tried as a medium of exchange.

Yap money stones

What's It Worth?

Unlike corn or salt or beads, most money has no value except as a medium of exchange. You can use a quarter to buy anything you want. Storekeepers use the quarters they get to buy anything they want. But the quarter has no other use except as a medium of exchange.

So why does our money work? It works because we all agree that it works. We agree that money has value. What if people decided that it didn't have value? Then our money wouldn't be worth a cent!

I get it! If it rains a lot, umbrellas become more valuable.

Not if you're a dog! Bones are more valuable than umbrellas!

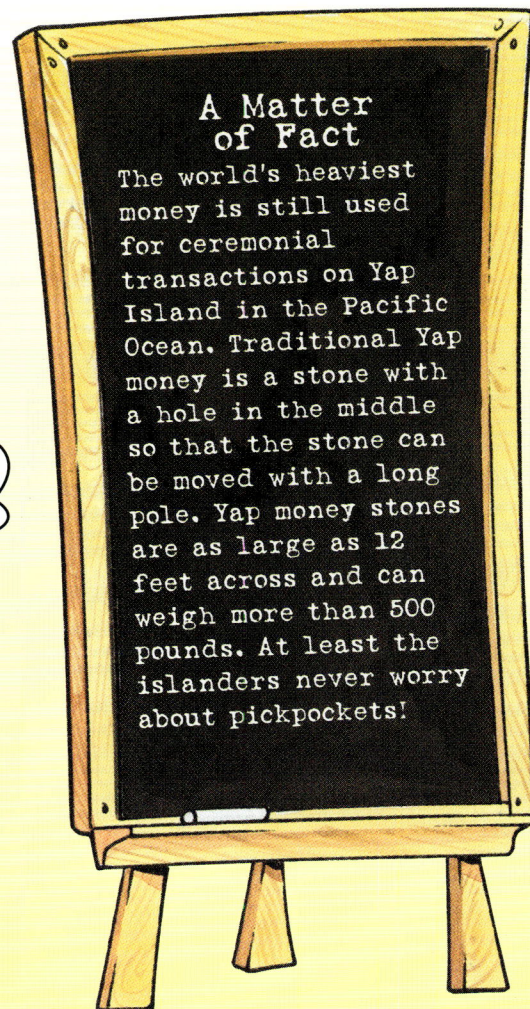

A Matter of Fact

The world's heaviest money is still used for ceremonial transactions on Yap Island in the Pacific Ocean. Traditional Yap money is a stone with a hole in the middle so that the stone can be moved with a long pole. Yap money stones are as large as 12 feet across and can weigh more than 500 pounds. At least the islanders never worry about pickpockets!

9

Coining Coins

Metal-ing in Money

But many mediums of exchange didn't work out so well. Feathers or seeds blew away. Barley spoiled. Camels were hard to move. Merchants needed a medium of exchange that was small, easy to handle and carry, and strong enough to last. They wanted something that people everywhere would accept in trade. They began to use **precious metals** as money.

Precious metals, like gold and silver, were hard to find. They were, therefore, valuable. Money made from these metals was accepted by many people because everybody wanted precious metals.

All That Glitters . . .

When people first decided that metal was the best material to use for money, they tended to use the metals found locally. These metals varied from place to place. Gold, silver, bronze, copper, and iron were the most common metals used, but lead and tin were also used.

Later, money made of gold and silver became the most valuable of all metal money. The people who used these metals weighed pieces of gold and silver to decide how much they were worth. Some early metal money was shaped into specially designed pellets or trinkets that were given a certain value.

A Penny for Your Thoughts

What is good about using a natural item as a medium of exchange? What problems might occur with their use?

Gold nugget and silver ore

Word Bank

precious metals *metals, such as gold and silver, that are valuable because they are rare*

Penny and Greek obela

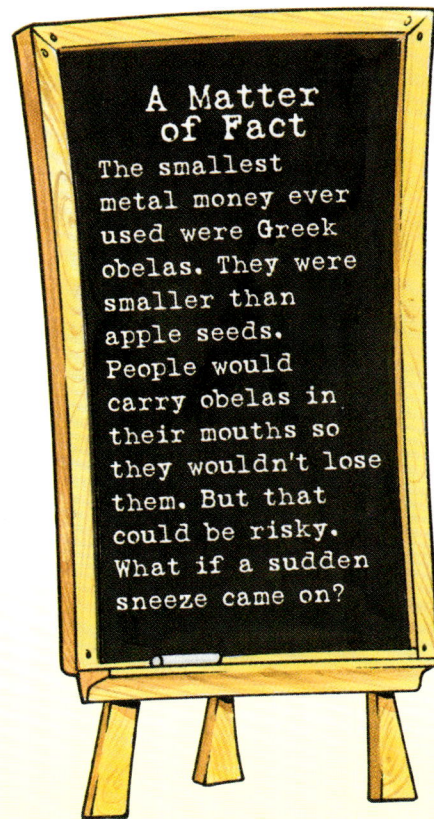

The First Coins

No one knows for sure who the first people were to use coins. Some people think it was the Sumerians, an ancient people who lived in Mesopotamia (which is now part of Iraq and part of Syria) about 5,000 years ago. Others believe it was the people of Egypt, around 2500 B.C. These people melted and shaped silver into tiny bars. Each was then stamped with its weight and used as money.

By 700 B.C., each Greek city had its own distinct flat pieces of metal that were stamped with a picture or a design. These were the first true coins to be **minted**. By 500 B.C., coins were being used as money all over Greece and Rome.

Early Greek money

Word Bank

mint *to stamp coins out of metal; a place where the coins of a country are made*

11

Gold!

In 640 B.C., Lydia, an ancient kingdom in what is Turkey today, used **electrum** to make its coins. Electrum is a natural mixture of gold and silver that is often found in rivers. To honor the king of Lydia, the coins were stamped with a lion's head. Lydia was the first country to use gold in its money. Gold coins eventually became the most valuable of all metal money.

Because pure gold is very soft, it is often mixed with other metals to make it harder. This mixture is called an **alloy**. The amount of gold in an alloy is measured in karats. One karat is 1/24 of the alloy.

Gold keeps its value because of its scarcity. There are estimated to be about 95 tons of gold in the world. That much gold would create a cube that measured 19 yards on each side!

Karats

- Pure gold is 24-karat gold.

- 14-karat gold is 14 parts gold and 10 parts of a mixture of silver and copper.

- 18-karat gold is 18 parts gold and 6 parts of a mixture of silver and copper.

Gold and other precious metals are weighed in pennyweights. Twenty pennyweights equal one troy ounce. One troy ounce is equal to 1/12 of a pound.

I thought there were 16 ounces in a pound!

Word Bank

electrum a natural mixture of gold and silver

alloy a mixture of two or more metals

Making Change

Coins became popular with people, and their use spread throughout the world. Pictures of great leaders were often stamped on the faces of the coins. Symbols of a country, such as birds, flowers, or animals, were also included on coins.

The coins were made of many metals—gold, silver, copper, iron, and bronze. Coins came in many shapes and sizes, but most were round. Countries were proud of their coins.

Before long, money as we know it was being used in trade throughout Europe, Asia, and the Middle East. Metal money made trade with other countries easier. Everything had an agreed-upon value, with money as the common medium of exchange. There were a few new complications because not all towns and countries used the same money. But it was much better than bartering.

But bartering did not disappear entirely. At first, money was used only by wealthy people for paying taxes. For many day-to-day things, people still bartered. Workers were often paid for their services with food, clothing, or a place to live. Even today, people still barter.

Metal Money— A Bestseller

Metal money was very popular for several reasons.

1. It was easy to carry—no matter where you went!
2. It didn't wear out easily.
3. There was a limited supply—it didn't grow on trees! But there was still enough so it wouldn't run out.
4. It could be changed when necessary. One coin could have one value stamped on it and another coin could have another value. Old money could also be melted down to make new money.

There are! But those ounces are called avoirdupois ounces. They're the ounces we use when we weigh most things.

I knew that!

Avoirdupois ounces! Troy ounces! No matter how you weigh it—a pound is still a pound!

13

Out With the Gold,

Eureka!

About 2,000 years ago, the Chinese invented both paper and a printing process. They also invented paper money! China did not have a large enough supply of metals for making coins. Instead, they hit upon the idea of making money out of paper. Each paper note was guaranteed by the government to have a certain value. Paper money quickly became their medium of exchange!

Europe at that time was using only coins. So when the explorer Marco Polo returned to Italy from China in 1295, he brought back exciting news: China had been using paper money for hundreds of years! But Europeans couldn't understand how paper could be valuable. It took another 400 years before Europeans caught on and started making paper money of their own.

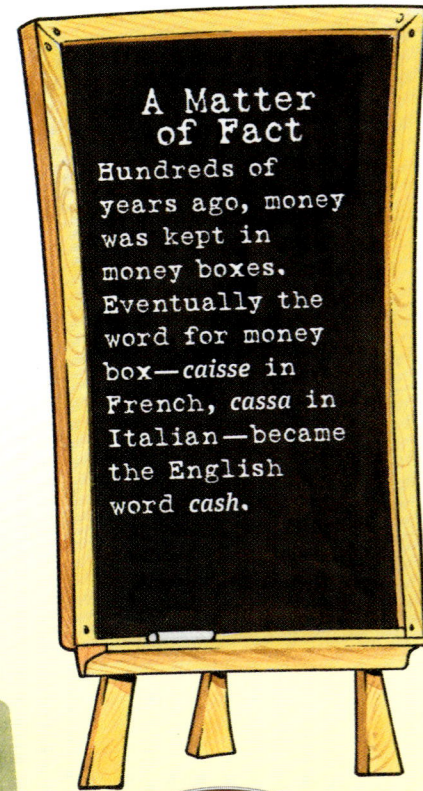

A Matter of Fact
Hundreds of years ago, money was kept in money boxes. Eventually the word for money box—*caisse* in French, *cassa* in Italian—became the English word *cash*.

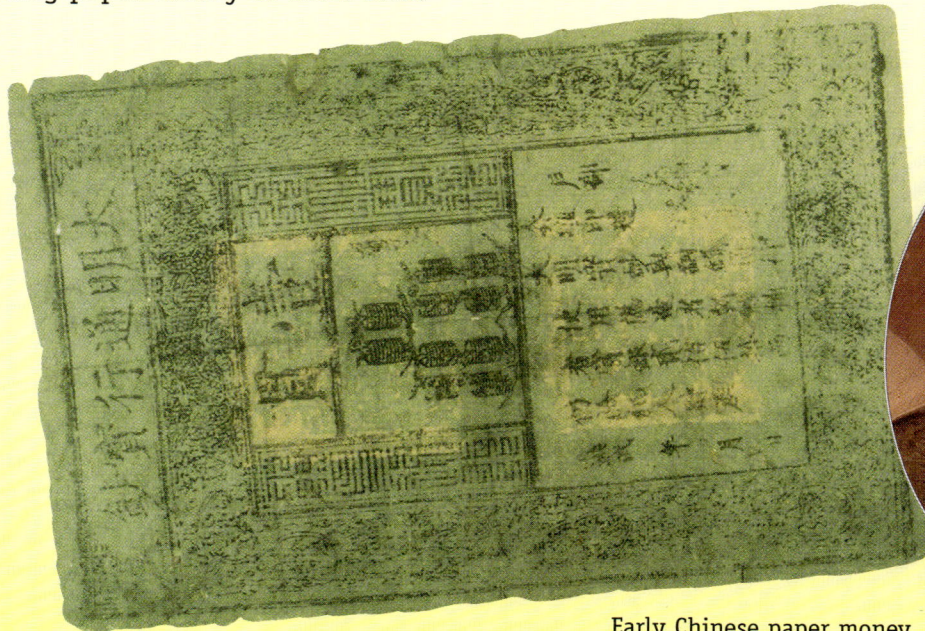

Early Chinese paper money

Marco Polo

14

In With the New

Guard Your Gold!

By the time of the Middle Ages in Europe (A.D. 800–1100), gold had become a popular medium for trade. But gold was heavy and difficult to carry. As only kings had access to safes, people often carried all their money around with them. That was a particular problem for wealthy people. Besides, streets and roads were not safe. It was dangerous to carry large amounts of gold.

The legend of Robin Hood began and spread quickly in the Middle Ages. He and his followers lived in the forest, stealing gold from the rich to give to the poor. To prevent people from having to carry so much gold, merchants and goldsmiths started issuing notes, promising to pay gold to the person carrying the note. These **promissory notes** were the beginning of paper money in Europe.

Before Its Time

Still, people in Europe felt safer using coins. Gold and silver were precious metals that would never lose their value because they could always be melted down. In the Middle Ages, Europe was made up of many small states that were at constant war with one another. The people did not have enough confidence in their governments to trust paper money. In fact, it wasn't until 1661 that Sweden became the first European country to print money on paper.

Word Bank

promissory note   *a written promise to pay a sum of money*

A Penny for Your Thoughts

Coins are fairly easy to carry around, but if you have a lot of them, they can be very heavy! Paper money is much lighter to carry. It is also much cheaper to make than coins. What other benefits does paper money have over coins? What are the drawbacks?

15

Take Your Pick!

Worth His Weight in Gold

In Greek mythology, King Midas wished that everything he touched would turn to gold. He made a big mistake! Everything he touched turned to gold, including his food! Today, when someone is successful at making a lot of money, we say he or she has the "Midas touch."

Read the story of Midas yourself. Find out what happens in the end. What do you think the phrase "All that glitters is not gold" means?

Penny Power

Take ten pennies and arrange them in a triangle like this. Moving only three pennies, make the triangle point in the opposite direction.

Coining Phrases

Here are some common expressions relating to money. What does each expression mean? Can you think of more expressions related to money?

- *a dime a dozen*
- *easy money*
- *pocket money*
- *penny-wise and pound-foolish*
- *the buck stops here*
- *break the bank*
- *rolling in dough*

Weighty Question

Which weighs more—a pound of feathers or a pound of gold? Are you sure?

Chapter 2

Money
in America

It's made of **metal**.
It's **made** of paper.
It has **value**.

What was the first U.S. money called?
What did it look like?
How are coins made?
Why does a dollar bill look the way it does?
Why do dimes, quarters, and half dollars have ridges?

You'll find the answers to these questions and more in this chapter. You'll learn why Americans used foreign coins for years. You'll learn why early American paper money was called greenbacks. You'll learn how long it takes a dollar bill to wear out—and you'll learn what all the special symbols on money mean. When you're done, you'll be heads (and tails) more money-wise than you were before!

Money Way

Whose Money Is Whose?

In the 1500s and 1600s, long before our country was born, many European countries started colonies in North America. What money did the colonists use? They used money from the countries they came from: Spain, England, France, and Holland. Early colonists also used Native American wampum as money.

But the most widely used coins in the colonies were Spanish silver dollars, often called pieces of eight because they could be cut into eight pieces called bits. The word *bit* is from an Old English word meaning "piece or morsel." Today, some people still call a quarter "two bits." Until 1850, Spanish silver dollars were the most widely used coins in the world. Many countries even adopted these coins as their own **currency**, or official money.

Colonial Cash

Since there weren't enough coins in the British colonies, people started making their own money in the mid-1600s. They called their coins shillings (s), pence (p), and pounds (£) like the money used in England.

The first British colony to make coins was Massachusetts. The government of this colony minted threepence, sixpence, and shilling coins. One of the best-known coins was the Pine Tree Shilling. It was named after the design stamped on the head of the coin. Later, in 1690, the same colony started a bank and issued paper money in several **denominations,** from two shillings to five pounds.

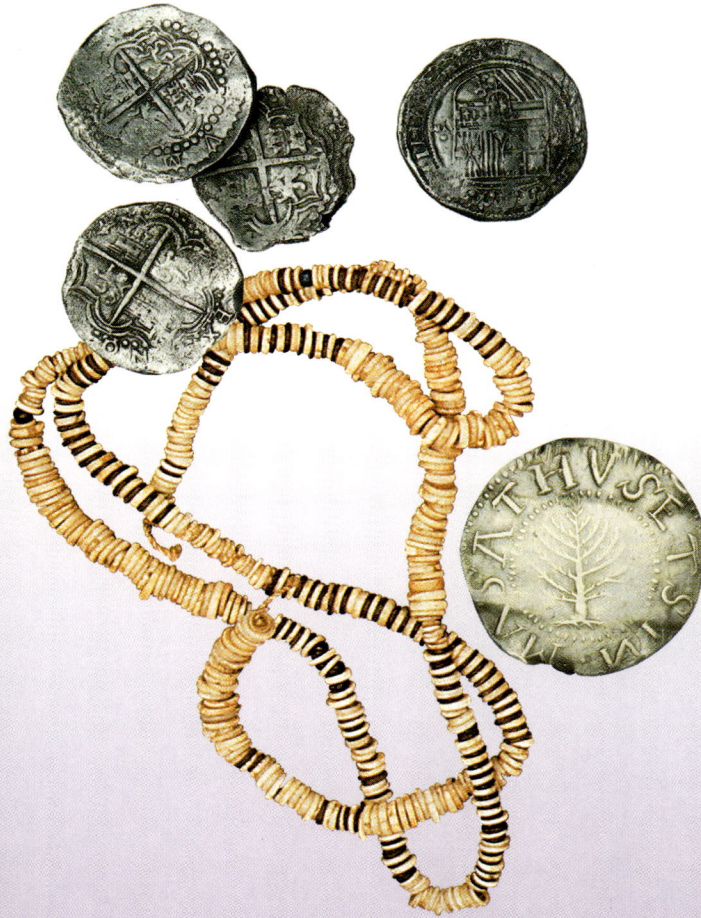

Early American money: pieces of eight, wampum, pine tree shilling

Word Bank

currency *any kind of money that is used as a medium of exchange*

denomination *bills of a particular value*

18

Back When

War Is Expensive!

When the colonies declared their freedom, or independence, from England, a war called the American Revolution began. The war lasted from 1775 to 1783. As you can imagine, paying soldiers and giving them clothing, food, shelter, and guns cost a lot—a lot more than the government had on hand. So it printed paper money, or notes, called **continentals**. When the government started running out of money, it printed more and more! When you print too much money, though, its value goes down. By 1783 a whole barrel of continentals couldn't buy a piece of cheese! After that, the government didn't issue paper money until the 1860s.

Franklin cent and a continental

A dollar gets its name from the German word Thaler, which was a large silver coin made in the Austrian town of Joachimsthaler.

Dollar sure is easier to say!

Not for me it isn't!

We Are Independent!

When the American Revolution ended, there were 13 different state currencies as well as foreign money in the new nation. So Congress decided that the states should all use the same currency. One of the first coins was minted in Connecticut in 1787. It showed 13 linked circles with one circle in the center with the words *United States* and *We are one*. Each circle represented one of the original 13 colonies.

In 1792, Congress passed a law establishing a new money system, with the dollar as the main unit of currency. The same law created the first national mint in Philadelphia, Pennsylvania. But why didn't the Americans just use the British system of pounds, shillings, and pence? Besides being the money system of the country the United States had just fought in a war, it was hard for the average person to understand. President Thomas Jefferson thought it would be easier for all Americans if our money were based on the decimal system. And that's what we still use today.

Word Bank
continental *paper money printed by Congress during the American Revolution*

19

Coins and More Coins

In 1793 newly minted cent and half-cent coins began rolling out of the Philadelphia Mint. Did you know that *cent* means $1/100$ of a unit, such as a dollar? Silver coins followed the next year, and gold coins the year after. The gold coins, called eagles, were produced until 1933. There were three different eagle coins, the $10.00 eagle, the $5.00 half eagle, and the $2.50 quarter eagle.

Even though America minted its own coins, foreign coins were still allowed to be used as money until 1857. But many Americans didn't like foreign currencies because there wasn't an agreed-upon value assigned to each coin. Imagine how difficult it would be to buy something if this were still true! Just try to buy those new sneakers you want with coins from ten different countries!

Early gold coins called "eagles"

A Penny for Your Thoughts

Suppose you could design a new coin. What would it be worth? What would it be made from? What would it look like? Whose picture would you put on it?

At Last!

At one time or another in the United States, there has been a 1/2-cent coin, a 2-cent coin, a 3-cent coin, and a 20-cent coin! Now that's UNcommon cents!

Take Note!

After the government's experience with continentals, only banks and private companies issued paper money, or notes. These notes promised that the bank would exchange the notes for either gold or silver. All was well until some banks ran out of gold or silver to exchange for the notes. So in 1861 the U.S. government stepped in and printed the first official United States paper money. These notes were called **greenbacks**.

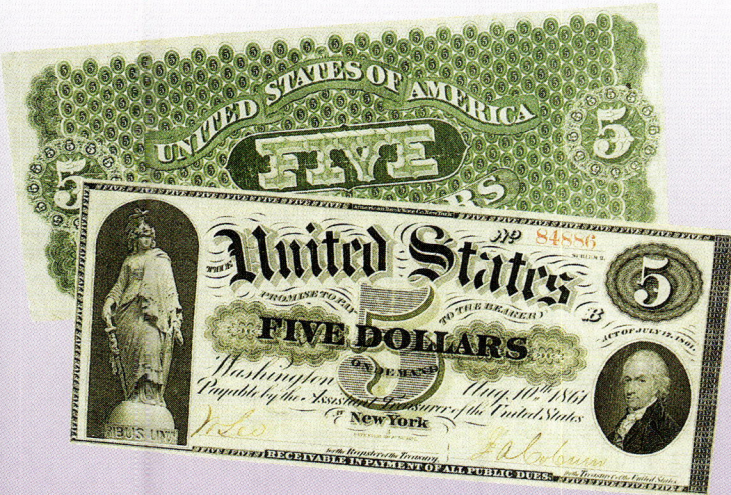

Greenbacks

Word Bank

greenbacks *the first official paper money printed by the U.S. government*

What a Mess!

Even though the government was printing its own money, banks were still allowed to print notes as long as they kept some money with the government. But this led to confusion. Banks in different states, and even banks in the same town, issued notes, or bills. Sometimes banks issued notes worth as little as 3 cents; sometimes the notes were worth a lot more. By 1863 there were thousands of notes in existence, all from different banks!

In 1913 the government stopped letting private banks print their own notes. The government bought all existing notes from the banks and a new system was started. It was about time! The government began issuing all paper money. This was the start of the notes and coins we use today.

A Matter of Fact

During the Civil War (1861–1865), people were afraid they wouldn't be able to exchange their paper money for gold or silver. To be safe, some people saved coins—lots of them. In fact, one house in New York City collapsed from the weight of the coins stored there!

21

Coins Up Close

I understand calling the faces of coins heads, but where did the term tails come from?

Tails refers to the bottom or back of coins.

Cool Mints!

The coins we use today are produced in U.S. government mints located in Denver, Colorado, and Philadelphia, Pennsylvania. The mint in Philadelphia is the largest in the world. When it is not busy minting American coins, it makes coins for other countries. The U.S. Mint is very busy—it produces about 13 billion coins per year!

How can you tell where a coin was minted? Look at the head of a coin such as a quarter. The tiny letter to the right of George Washington's head is called the mint mark. It tells you where the coin was minted. *P* stands for Philadelphia; *D* stands for Denver. If you see an *O* or an *S*, that's because there were once mints in New Orleans and San Francisco.

Making Coins

Today's coins are not made of gold or silver. They are made from copper and nickel alloys, which are cheaper and more available than precious metals.

To make coins, the metal is melted and poured into molds to make bars, or **ingots**. Machines roll the ingots into sheets. Blanks for each type of coin are punched from the sheets. They are then put through an edge-rolling machine, which produces a raised rim. Finally, the designs on both sides of the coin are stamped at the same time. All United States coins have two sayings stamped on them: E Pluribus Unum (which is Latin for "Out of many, one"), and In God We Trust. The completed coins are loaded into machines that automatically count them and drop them into bags, which are weighed and sent off to banks.

Word Bank

ingot *metal cast in a convenient shape before it is made into something else*

22

Mill-ions of Coins

Find a dime or a quarter and run your finger around the edge. Feel the ridges. Coins haven't always had ridges. **Milled coins**, coins with ridges, were created to solve a problem. When coins were still made from gold and silver, some people would shave the edges of the coins and sell the valuable scraps. Ridges were put on the edges of the coins to stop this. Even though quarters and dimes are no longer made of silver, they still have ridges around the edges.

A Dollar That Thinks It's a Quarter

In 1979 the United States minted a new one-dollar coin. On it was a picture of Susan B. Anthony, who fought for women's rights in the late 1800s. The government thought people would prefer the convenience of a dollar coin. However, it was too much like a quarter in size, and people were easily confused. Millions of Susan B. Anthony dollars were minted, but only a small number were circulated. Now the government has 400 million of these coins in storage!

A Penny for Your Thoughts

By law, money cannot show a living person. This law was passed so that no person could mint coins as a sign of power, as the English kings did. Do you think this is still a good idea?

Whose images are on the other sides of these coins?

1. penny
2. nickel
3. dime
4. quarter
5. half dollar

Word Bank

milled coins *coins with ridged edges*

1. Abraham Lincoln; 2. Thomas Jefferson; 3. Franklin D. Roosevelt; 4. George Washington; 5. John F. Kennedy

The Paper Chase!

Pressing Issues

All paper money is printed at the Bureau of Engraving and Printing in Washington, D.C. That's where postage stamps are also printed. What do you think paper money is made from? If you said paper, you're wrong! It is made from a special blend of 25% cotton and 75% linen, which lasts longer. It is against the law to make this special blend without permission from the Bureau of Engraving and Printing. About 30 bills can be printed on a single sheet of paper. After the bills are printed, they are cut apart, pressed, starched, and bundled.

No Faking!

To stop people from making **counterfeit,** or fake, money, bills are made in a very particular way. Each bill has a serial number printed on it for identification. The serial numbers are recorded so the government knows exactly which bills are in circulation. There are different inks used to print bills, but only one company has the special secret formulas for making them. Also, even though you can't see them, there are red and blue fibers, or threads, running through each bill.

Can bills be washed, too?

Sure they can. It's called laundering money!

Word Bank

counterfeit *to make a copy of something that people will think is genuine*

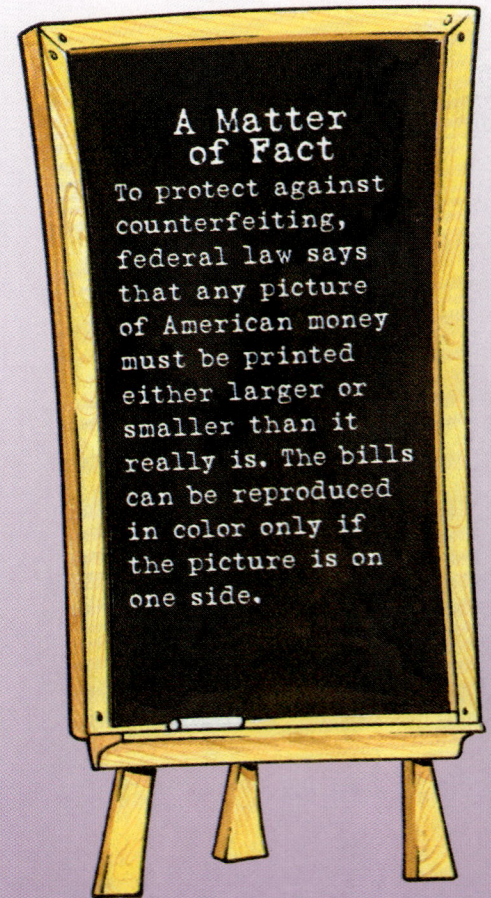

A Matter of Fact

To protect against counterfeiting, federal law says that any picture of American money must be printed either larger or smaller than it really is. The bills can be reproduced in color only if the picture is on one side.

Did you ever really take a good look at a dollar bill? Try it! What do you see?

1 This mark tells you which Federal Reserve Bank first issued the bill.

A Boston
B New York
C Philadelphia
D Cleveland
E Richmond
F Atlanta
G Chicago
H St. Louis
I Minneapolis
J Kansas City
K Dallas
L San Francisco

2 This is the serial number of the bill. Every bill has a different number.

3 This is the signature of the treasurer of the United States at the time the bill is printed.

4 This shows the date that this bill design was first used.

5 This is the great seal of the United States. The unfinished pyramid symbolizes growth. The eye represents the watchful gaze of God.

6 The eagle, the symbol of the United States, stands for strength. Thirteen stars and stripes stand for the first 13 states.

7 The olive branch stands for peace. The arrows show that Americans will fight to defend themselves.

25

Big Bucks!

The largest denomination of a bill ever printed in the United States was the $100,000 bill. Imagine making change for that! Actually, the $100,000 bill was used only to make payments between banks. For a while the Bureau of Engraving and Printing made $500; $1,000; $5,000; and $10,000 bills. Since very few people used them, they are no longer made. Today the largest bill in circulation is the $100 bill.

Do you know whose portraits belong on these bills?

Maybe someday my face will appear on a bill!

But you won't get to see it—you have to be dead to have your face on a coin or bill.

Keeping Count

The government keeps careful track of how much money is made and used. When paper money gets too old or worn, it's taken out of circulation. Then the money is shredded. It used to be burned, but this practice was stopped because of the pollution this caused. The average life of a dollar bill is 18 months, but a $50 bill lasts 9 years!

Every day the Bureau of Printing and Engraving receives thousands of bills that have been badly mangled or destroyed. Most of them are replaced with new bills. The Bureau has received money that had been stuffed in mattresses, chewed by mice, burned, and buried. It has even received money chewed by cows!

A Matter of Fact
In 1995 it cost 4 cents to make one bill. In that year 9.7 billion bills were produced!

26

$1–George Washington; $5–Abraham Lincoln; $10–Alexander Hamilton

Guarding the Gold

As you might remember reading, our dollars used to be backed by gold. That meant that you could bring paper money to a bank and exchange it for an equal amount of gold. This kind of money system is called a **gold standard**. But as the government got stronger, our currency did, too. There was no longer any need to back paper money with gold. In 1971 the United States officially abandoned the gold standard.

Without the gold standard the amount of money in circulation can be controlled without worrying about how much gold there is. However, the government still owns billions of dollars' worth of gold, stored at Fort Knox, Kentucky. The gold ingots stored there are locked inside concrete and steel vaults. The building is bombproof and is protected by many alarms and armed security guards. And it's never been broken into!

Around the World

As you learned earlier, the official unit of currency in the United States is the dollar. But most every country in the world has its own official unit of currency. In France the official currency is the franc, in Germany it is the mark, in Japan the yen, and in India the rupee. There are about 140 different currencies in use today around the world.

Most countries make their own money. Each country has its own special ink and paper. Each country has secret formulas and processes for coining and printing money. All the same coins and bills must match in size, weight, and appearance. Money all over the world is made very, *very* carefully.

A Penny for Your Thoughts

What problems do you think are caused by having so many different currencies around the world? Are there any advantages?

Word Bank

gold standard *the system of currency in which paper money can be exchanged for a fixed amount of gold*

Take Your Pick!

Make Your Moves

Rearrange the coins so that the pennies are in boxes 4 and 5 and the nickels are in boxes 1 and 2.

- You may slide a coin into an empty box.
- You may jump over a coin and land in an empty box.
- You may have only one coin in a box at a time.

Use real coins and a grid like the one shown. Can you make the switch in eight moves?

1	2	3	4	5

In Mint Condition

Naming Coins

Your friend has 5 coins. The average value of the coins is 11¢. What coins does your friend have?

On a typical day the United States Mint makes
451,000,000 pennies
2,000,000 nickels
10,000,000 dimes
4,000,000 quarters
120,000 half dollars . . .

That's a BIG pile of money! I wonder how much money (in dollars) the mint makes every day.

For that matter, how much money is that in 1 year? (If the mint is open 257 days per year?)

More than I can carry!

It's Your Money!

What will you do with it?
How can you use
it wisely?

From beads to bank notes, money has changed a lot. Now that you know a little about the history of money, it's time to decide how to earn it, save it, spend it, and share it!

The easy part is spending it. You—along with all the other kids across America—spend billions of dollars a year. You buy food and drinks. You buy tapes and CDs. You buy clothing and movie tickets. You may even have a say in the food your family buys or the vacations you may take.

How do most people get their money?
What do they spend it on?
What's the best way to manage money?

In Chapter 3, you'll find the answers to these questions—and more. You'll pick up some shopping tips. You'll understand how to budget. In short, you'll be getting valuable ideas on how to get the most for your money.

29

Making Money

Do You Yearn to Earn?

Have you ever heard the saying *Money doesn't grow on trees*? If the answer is yes, then you probably understand that you often need to earn the money that you spend. Any money that you earn or receive from someone else is called **income**. There are many different kinds of income. You can earn money doing a job such as watching pets, baby-sitting, or raking leaves. You can also earn money by keeping it in a bank. Even gifts of money from relatives count as income!

Word Bank

income *the money a person gets from salary or wages, interest, investments, and other sources*

wages *money paid to an employee for work done*

employee *a person who works for another in return for pay*

employer *a person or company for whom other people work for pay*

salary *a fixed amount of money paid regularly for work done*

Bringing Home the Bacon

Do you have an income now? Some kids earn an allowance by doing chores, such as helping with the laundry, taking care of a pet, or cleaning up after meals. Some kids work outside their homes for extra cash. They may get paid money, or **wages**, from a business or a shopkeeper. But most kids your age like being in business for themselves. Have you ever had a lemonade stand or made something else to sell? If so, you've been a small-business owner.

Most adults get their money by working for it. People work for another person, a business, or the government. Or they run their own business. A person who works for someone else is called an **employee**. The person or company that an employee works for is an **employer**. An employer pays a **salary**, or a fixed sum of money, to its employees on a regular basis. Some people who are unable to earn enough income to survive receive help from the government to pay their bills. This kind of help is called welfare.

If you work for someone and you have somebody working for you, you are both an employee and an employer!

Even if you're a dog?

30

What's in a Job?

Plenty! Have you ever thought about the kind of job you'd like when you're an adult? As you can see in the chart below, some jobs require more schooling or special training than others. As a result, many workers in such jobs earn higher salaries. Do you see on the chart a job that you're interested in? Can you think of more jobs to add?

What would you like to be when you grow up? To help you decide, you might talk to people about their work. What skills do they have? How did their interests as a young person affect their job decisions? What special schooling or training was needed for them to become successful? What makes them want to go to work every day, besides the salary? Remember, it's important to enjoy the work you do.

Everything Changes

For hundreds—even thousands—of years, people have worked at different jobs. But jobs have changed over the years, and some have completely disappeared, such as lamplighter, iceman, and town crier. Other jobs have been modernized. For example, today's air-mail pilot has replaced the pony express rider. And some jobs didn't even exist twenty years ago! Below are some of the fastest-growing occupations in the United States today.

Fastest-growing Occupations

Health and medical field:	physicians, medical assistants, technicians
Computer science:	computer programmers, scientists, systems analysts
Human services:	social workers, child-care workers, chefs, cooks, gardeners
Travel:	flight attendants, travel agents
Teaching:	elementary school teachers, high school teachers

Job Training/Schooling and Salary

Job	Recommended Training/Schooling	Average Yearly Salary (1996)
Airline pilot	4 years of college and flight experience	$96,000
Auto mechanic	1 year of training	$24,000
Carpenter	3 to 4 years of training	$25,000
High school teacher	4 or 5 years of college	$36,000
Lawyer	4 years of college and 3 years of law school	$59,000
Physician	4 years of college and 4 years of medical school	$156,000

A Penny for Your Thoughts

Many jobs today couldn't have been imagined 100 years ago—even by science-fiction writers! Which jobs today do you think didn't exist 100 years ago? What do you think jobs in the future might be like?

31

Dollars and Sense

Have you bought an ice-cream cone lately? Some sports equipment? Have you phoned a friend or gone to the movies? If you answered yes to any of these, you are a **consumer**—someone who uses or consumes goods and services. A **producer**, on the other hand, is someone who makes goods or provides services. A producer may make the food you buy or serve you dinner at your favorite restaurant.

It's very easy to be a consumer. Anyone who has money to spend can be one. But it takes effort and know-how to be a smart consumer.

Gosh! I grew my own vegetables and now I'm eating them. That makes me both a producer and a consumer.

Hello to "Good Buys"

Which of the following statements are true?
  A. *The size of a package tells you how much is inside.*
  B. *The more gadgets an appliance has, the better it will work.*
  C. *The best value is always a well-known brand.*

The above statements are all false! Are you surprised? Being a smart consumer is not always easy. It takes some work. One way to get the most for your dollar is to be a **comparison shopper**. That means you compare the different brands of a product as you shop. Read labels. Check ingredients. Look for the weight of the contents, not the size of the package. Compare prices and quality. Sometimes a product that costs more may be a better deal if it is made to last longer or comes with a better **warranty**. A warranty guarantees that the company that made the product—or the business that sold it—will fix or replace it if anything goes wrong, within a certain period of time.

Word Bank

consumer *someone who buys and uses goods and services*

producer *the person or business that provides goods and services*

comparison shopper *one who examines products to see how they are alike or different*

warranty *a written guarantee to repair or replace a product if something goes wrong within a limited period of time*

32

Does It Go?

The "Buy" Line

What costs hundreds of thousands of dollars, lasts 30 seconds, and is seen by millions of people? A TV commercial. Advertisers spend a lot of money "selling" products on TV. Ads can be useful to consumers. They can tell you about a product, a service, or a company. They can make you see something in a new way. But ads can also be misleading if you don't understand their purpose. They can make you want to buy or use something for the wrong reasons.

A Matter of Fact

On January 27, 1991, Super Bowl XXV was watched by over 120 million viewers. For a 30-second television commercial during that game, advertisers had to pay $800,000!

You have to sell a lot of stuff to meet those kinds of expenses!

Save, Spend, or Give?

When you have money, the first choice you need to make is whether or not to spend it. How much you save is up to you. How much you spend and how you spend it is also up to you. In general, people use money to buy the things they **need**, such as shoes or food, or **want**, such as a new soccer ball or computer game. But money can also be used for other things. For example, you might want to buy someone a present or **donate** money to a worthy cause or charity.

The choices people make about money are very personal. What's important to one person may not be as important to another. People have different ideas about needs and wants. To one family, having a car may be a necessity. To another, it may be viewed as a luxury. The key to being a smart consumer is knowing what's important to you—and why. What are the things you really couldn't live without? What things would be nice to have but are not necessary for your survival?

Word Bank

need *something that you must have*

want *something that you would like to have but don't necessarily need*

donate *to contribute money, a gift, or time to a worthy cause, fund, or charity*

33

Saving and Spending

The Ins and Outs of Managing Money

Where does your money go? That is one of the most important questions you have to ask yourself once you have money of your own to spend and save. Keeping track of how much you have and what you are spending it on—and knowing whether or not you can afford to buy what you want—are the secrets to success with money.

A **budget** can help you manage your money. A budget is a plan that shows how much money comes in and how much money goes out. Keeping a record of your income and spending can provide you with useful information. It can help you plan for the future. You might spot places you can cut spending in order to have more money for other things.

There are two parts to any budget.

Part 1: Money In

This part of your budget shows your income, or the money you get from your allowance, gifts, and jobs. Your income may vary from week to week.

Part 2: Money Out

This part of your budget shows how you use your money. It includes spending, savings, and if you choose, donating.

Spending includes everything you need to spend money on, such as bus fare or lunch. It covers those extras, too—the things you buy just because you want them, such as snacks or movie tickets.

Savings is money you put away to use later on. Savings can help you plan for buying things you know you will need or want in the future. Short-term savings is money saved to buy something in the near future, like a book. Medium-term savings is money you save over a longer period of time, probably to buy a more expensive item, like a bike. You also have to think about long-term savings, or money you save for the distant future, as for college. It could take you years to save for that!

> I saved money by building a bookcase out of orange crates.

> How clever! What will you do next?

> Try to figure out a way to get rid of all those oranges!

Word Bank

budget *a plan of how much money a person, business, government, or organization has to spend and how it will be spent*

34

What's the Plan?

How It's Done

Look at Marta's weekly budget. What do you notice about how Marta manages money? If you noticed she doesn't spend more than she has, you'd be right. That's the sign of a good budget!

> Managing money can be simple once you understand that what you have to spend is all you have to spend.

> With empty pockets, I'm not going to be spending very much!

MARTA'S WEEKLY BUDGET

Money In

Income	
allowance	$7.00
gift from Uncle Joe	3.00
Total	$10.00

Money Out

Spending	
snack	$2.50
pen	.50
baseball cards	2.00
Savings (for bike)	$3.00
Sharing	
UNICEF donation	$2.00
Total	$10.00

Get On Track

One good way to avoid running out of money is to have a weekly spending plan, like Marta's, and stick to it. The steps outlined below will help you.

- List all your income—all the money coming in.
- List all the things you spend money on regularly—for example, bus fare and snack. Include any new expense you expect during the week, such as a birthday present, and estimate the amount. That money is for "extras."
- Think about what you're saving for. Write the amount you need to put aside each week to make this happen.
- Finally, list any donations you might make to help others.
- Now you can subtract the *money out* from the *money in*. Your budget should balance.

All in the Family

Do you know where your family's income comes from? Do you know what your family spends money on? The chart below shows Marta's family's budget. It includes typical expenses for her family.

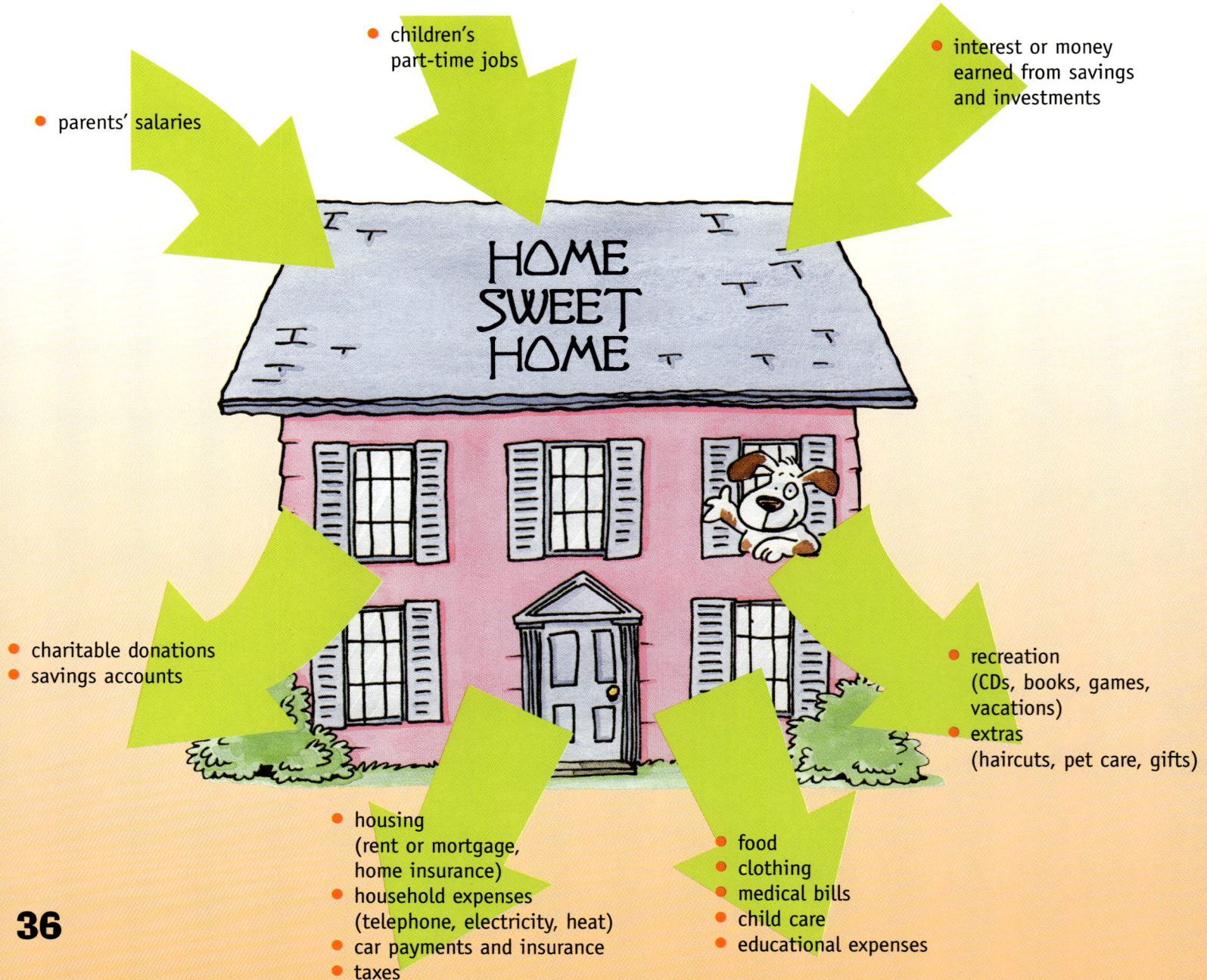

- children's part-time jobs
- interest or money earned from savings and investments
- parents' salaries

HOME
SWEET
HOME

- charitable donations
- savings accounts

- recreation (CDs, books, games, vacations)
- extras (haircuts, pet care, gifts)

- housing (rent or mortgage, home insurance)
- household expenses (telephone, electricity, heat)
- car payments and insurance
- taxes

- food
- clothing
- medical bills
- child care
- educational expenses

36

Budgeting—
It's All Around You!

So now that you know how to budget, you might be surprised to learn how many people are **balancing budgets**, or trying to make sure that the money going out is equal to or less than the money coming in. Not only do individuals and families budget, but businesses, organizations (like the Girl Scouts or UNICEF) and even governments budget, too. Wherever there's money, it has to be managed. And it should be managed wisely.

A Penny for Your Thoughts

What if your family decided to go on a weekend trip? Where would you go? What would you see and do? How much would it cost? Where would the money come from to pay for it? How could you cut costs?

Word Bank

balanced budget *a budget in which the money going out is equal to or less than the money taken in*

opportunity cost *the cost of what you are giving up to get something you want more*

It's a Choice!

One thing is for sure—budgeting involves making choices. You have to choose what to do with your money. How much should you save? How much should you spend? What should you spend it on? What are you willing to give up to get what you want? The cost of your decision is called an **opportunity cost**. The opportunity cost is what you are giving up. Suppose you want to buy a T-shirt and a CD, but you only have enough money to buy one item. If you decide to buy the CD, the opportunity cost, or what you are giving up, is the T-shirt. Can you think of some choices you've made lately? What did you give up to get what you wanted? Was it worth it?

So, What Do You Think?

Is spending as easy as you thought it was? It really takes a lot of work to spend wisely. You need to think about what you want today as well as what you want tomorrow.

37

Take Your Pick!

Time to Budget

Make up a monthly budget based on your allowance or on an allowance of $5 per week. How much would you save? How much would you spend? If you were saving up for a compact disc, how long do you think it would take you? What if you were saving up to buy a computer game?

Shop 'Til You Drop

Congratulations! You've just won a *million* dollars! How long would it take you to spend all that money if you shopped 24 hours a day and spent $200 every minute? What do you think you would buy (in one minute) for $200?

Mind Your Business!

If you need extra cash, you could start your own business. What product would you sell? Would you provide a service instead? Come up with a catchy slogan to sell your product or service. Maybe you could even write a little jingle!

Party!

You've come to the end of the chapter. Time to celebrate! Suppose you had $50 to spend on a party. Make a plan. Where will your party be? How many friends will you invite? What will you do? What will you eat? What will you buy with your $50?

Glossary

alloy a mixture of two or more metals

balanced budget a budget in which the money going out is equal to or less than the money taken in

barter trading goods or services with someone for different goods or services, without using money

budget a plan of how much money a person, business, government, or organization is able to spend and how it will be spent

comparison shopper one who examines products to see how they are alike or different

consumer someone who buys and uses goods and services

continentals paper money printed by Congress during the American Revolution

counterfeit to make a copy of something that people will think is genuine

currency any kind of money that is used as a medium of exchange

denomination bills of a particular value

dollar the official unit of currency in the United States; based on the decimal system

donate to contribute money, a gift, or time to a worthy cause, fund, or charity

electrum a natural mixture of gold and silver

employee a person who works for another in return for pay

employer a person or company for whom other people work for pay

gold standard the system of currency in which paper money can be exchanged for a fixed amount of gold

goods real items, such as cars, wristwatches, and clothing

greenbacks the first official paper money printed by the U.S. government

income the money a person gets from salary or wages, profits, interest, investments, and other sources

ingot metal cast in a convenient shape before it is made into something else

medium of exchange anything that a group of people agree has a certain worth

milled coin a coin with ridged edges

mint to stamp coins out of metal; a place where the coins of a country are made

money anything a group of people accept in exchange for goods and services

need something that you must have

opportunity cost the cost of what you are giving up to get something you want more

precious metals metals, such as gold and silver, that are valuable because they are rare

producer a person or business that provides goods and services

promissory note a written promise to pay a sum of money

salary a fixed amount of money paid regularly for work done, usually a yearly rate of pay

services work that is done for other people; for example, work done by waiters, lawyers, and nurses

taxes money that a government collects from people and businesses

value the worth of something as measured in goods, services, or a medium of exchange

wages money paid to an employee for work done; may be an hourly rate of pay

want something that you would like to have but don't necessarily need

warranty a written guarantee to repair or replace a product if something goes wrong within a limited period of time

welfare income paid by the government to people who need it to live

41

Index